Original title:
A Necklace for Every Heart

Copyright © 2025 Creative Arts Management OÜ
All rights reserved.

Author: Lorenzo Barrett
ISBN HARDBACK: 978-1-80586-081-5
ISBN PAPERBACK: 978-1-80586-553-7

The Essence of Togetherness

In a drawer, sparkles hide,
Each one holds a tale inside.
Brother's charm, a cat's big grin,
Sister's gem, lost in the din.

Necklace made of bits and bobs,
Fashioned from our quirky jobs.
Mom's ring, locks of dad's gray hair,
A necklace? No! A family fair!

Emblems of Our Souls

Boasting beads from times gone by,
Each one whispers, 'Oh, my my!'
Uncle's button, fierce and bold,
A fashion statement worth its gold.

Cousin's knick-knack, wobbly, weird,
Finders keepers, no one cheered.
A trinket here, a token there,
Our jewelry's an eclectic dare!

Hues of Harmony

Colors clash like moods at noon,
Laughter rises, a funny tune.
Orange, purple, green, and blue,
All together in a stew.

If chaos wore a shining crown,
This bling's the goofiest around!
A pendant shaped like mom's old shoe,
Who knew mismatched could feel brand new?

A Chain of Memories

Link by link, our stories grow,
Every charm, a secret show.
Gramps' watch, mischief in the air,
Caught the time but lost his hair!

Every jingle sings a song,
A history where we belong.
From every laugh, a charm doth spring,
Oh, the joy that memories bring!

Jewels of Emotion

In the drawer, they sit and gleam,
A gem of laughter, a sparkling dream.
Each twinkle, a chuckle, a wink so bright,
Worn at parties, they steal the night.

A ruby grin, a sapphire jest,
Put them on, and you're dressed best!
With every sparkle, a story told,
Of love and mischief, both bold and gold.

Threads of Connection

With ribbons of joy, we tie them tight,
A string of giggles, oh what a sight!
Worn by friends who know the score,
They gather around, laughing more and more.

Like beaded tales, they interlace,
In every knot, there's a smiling face.
A friendship bracelet, a shared delight,
Together we shine, so bright, so right!

Adornments of Affection

A brooch of banter, a pin of play,
With every pin, we brighten the day.
Silly charms stacked high and proud,
Making faces in a colorful crowd.

These trinkets jingle, these baubles buzz,
Like secret whispers and cheerful fuzz.
With every clasp, a giggle ensues,
Our hearts adorned with colorful hues.

Pendants of the Soul

With pendants swinging, we chase the fun,
Each laughter echo, a race that's won.
From dangles to charms, they sway in glee,
As we bump and wiggle, wild and free.

A locket laughs, a chain of cheer,
Holding memories we love and hold dear.
Around our necks, this laughter flies,
A carnival of joy beneath the skies.

Reflections of Affection

In a jewel box, shiny and bright,
I found a trinket that gave me a fright.
It shimmered and sparkled with every twist,
But on closer look, it was hard to resist.

There's one shaped like a pickle, believe it or not,
Next to a donut, it's quite the hot spot.
A taco charm winks, oh what a delight,
I can wear them all out, just not overnight!

My friends laugh and point, calling me queen,
With food on my chest, it's a sight to be seen!
I strut down the street with my bling and my flair,
Fashion advice? I don't really care!

So here's to the odd, the weird and the fun,
Each quirky piece, my laughter's begun.
For every attachment that makes people cheer,
I'll wear all my charms, while sipping on beer!

Charms of Memory

A charm of laughter, so delightfully bold,
Hanging with stories, both new and old.
Each jingle a giggle, a tickle in time,
Its shiny reflection, a glittering rhyme.

What's this one here? A slice of pie?
It didn't last long, oh my, oh my!
A charm for the hiccups that make us bright,
It glows in the dark, a true joyful sight.

Beads of Emotion

Stringing together our moments so sweet,
This bead of regret feels like wet, soggy feet.
Next comes the joy, all sparkly and round,
It dances and shimmies, it's never quite bound.

A bead of confusion, a tangle of strings,
Makes us all giggle with the chaos it brings.
Together we laugh, through smiles and through tears,
These beads of our life, like colorful years.

Elegance Woven in Love

In a fabric of fun, with threads made of cheer,
We weave our odd stories, like socks without leer.
A twist of some kindness, a dash of good vibes,
With loops of sweet laughter, our hearts shall imbibe.

Patterns of pie and some chocolate delight,
In elegance woven, we shine oh so bright.
Who needs fancy jewels, when silliness reigns?
Our tapestry sparkles through mischief and gains.

Trinkets of Togetherness

A trinket of friendship, a goofy charade,
With secrets to share, and plans we have made.
An inside joke, like a bright, funny hat,
Together we sparkle, where giggles are at.

Look at this bauble; it jangles with fun,
It's from that wild moment, we raced just for pun.
These trinkets unite us, like glue for the soul,
In our treasure-filled antics, we make each other whole.

Talismans of Togetherness

In this quirky jewelry shop,
You'll find a slinky bangle,
One for the giggles,
And another for the jangle.

There's a charm for the awkward,
With a spin and a twist,
It's the perfect gift,
For when you can't resist.

Like beads of laughter strung,
On a chain of silly pranks,
Each piece a story told,
In the voice of the hijinks.

So wear them all at once,
Let them dance and sing,
With every clink and clank,
You'll feel the joy they bring.

Gemstones of Memories

A ruby for the blunders,
Emeralds for the fun,
Sapphires for the late-night chats,
And laughter that weighs a ton.

Each gem a silly story,
A fractured fairy tale,
Bouncing from the past,
With every twist and flail.

The diamonds slip and slide,
On the floors of our delight,
A sparkling floor of memories,
That twinkle through the night.

So gather all your trinkets,
Polish up that shine,
For every laugh we've shared,
Is a reason to align.

Heartstrings Entwined

With threads of colored yarn,
We weave a playful bind,
Each loop a tale of mishaps,
In the laughter we unwind.

A button pops, a bead rolls,
Watch them bounce away,
But every string that tangles,
Brings memories to play.

In this circus of colors,
Our hearts dance a wild jig,
With every twist and shout,
We're living like a big pig.

So tie that ribbon tightly,
And let it spin and twine,
In the antics of our hearts,
We've made a grand design.

Tokens of Tenderness

A paperclip as a token,
For all the notes we've shared,
A token of affection,
For each time that we dared.

With spoons from every dinner,
And forks for all the cake,
Each piece a little reminder,
Of love we dared to bake.

The goofy gifts we treasure,
With smiles from ear to ear,
They're the tokens from our journey,
In all the laughter shared near.

So celebrate those moments,
With winks and silly cheer,
For every quirky treasure,
Is the joy that draws us near.

Luminescence of Love

In a box full of gems, oh what a sight,
A crooked little charm, not quite upright.
It sparkles with laughter, and joy it conveys,
Like socks on a dog, it brightens our days.

Mismatched and silly, yet all of us know,
Together we're stronger, we steal the show.
With glittering giggles, we jump and we swirl,
Adorning each moment, we dance and we twirl.

The Spark of Unity

A button and thread, a banana in tow,
Crafting a masterpiece, an offbeat show!
With laughter as glue, we stitch it just right,
Creating a tapestry, a dazzling sight.

Through picnics and puddles, we jump in delight,
Mixing up colors, oh, what a sight!
We chuckle at chaos, embrace it with zest,
Together we shine, bright hearts on a quest.

Pieces of Us

A cupcake and sprinkles, a hat that's too wide,
We wear our odd choices, with giggles and pride.
When friends craft a treasure, from pieces so small,
It's charmingly quirky, the best gift of all.

Like mismatched socks dancing, together we sway,
With a wink and a nudge, we brighten the day.
Each quirk a connection, we share with a grin,
In the patchwork of friendship, we'll always win!

Hues of Heartfelt Moments

A rainbow of laughter, oh what a paint,
With friends by our side, we feel like a saint.
Like crayons misplaced in a colorful spree,
Each hue tells a story, vibrant and free.

Silly and sunny, we splash through the rain,
In this joyful madness, we find the mundane.
With chuckles like fireworks, our hearts start to race,
In the hues of our memories, we find our place.

Heartfelt Echoes

In the drawer, a treasure lies,
With charms that giggle, spark, and rise.
A rubber chicken, a heart-shaped wing,
It tells a tale only laughter can bring.

In mismatched pairs, the trinkets jive,
Like dancing penguins, oh, how they thrive!
A necklace made of spaghetti dreams,
Swings to the rhythm of silly screams.

Bonds Beneath the Surface

Underneath the sofa, a charm brigade,
Comes to life in a colorful parade.
A donut pendant and a fish-shaped dude,
With their silly faces, they change the mood.

Together they strut, with flair and delight,
Turning serious moments into pure light.
With every giggle, a bond we create,
Wearing joy like a necklace that won't wait.

Layers of Love

A necklace of laughter, a loop of cheer,
With jelly beans hanging, how lovely, my dear!
Each layer a story, a prank or a pun,
With sparkly sequins that always run.

When life starts to frown, we just give a twirl,
Our silly accessories make the world swirl.
A smile's the gem that lights up the scene,
With layers of wonders, we laugh in between.

A Gallery of Affections

In an artful display, there lives a mix,
Of buttons and fumbles, and thrift store picks.
A canvas of chaos, a rainbow of glee,
Each charm is a memory of you and me.

A quirky design that tickles the eye,
With a paperclip pendant that whispers, "Oh my!"
In this gallery of treasures, we find our way,
Fashioning laughter for each goofy day.

An Embrace in Every Stone

In a world where sparkles play,
There's a gem for every day.
When I wear my finest bead,
I feel like royalty with speed.

Beads of laughter, laid in rows,
Oh, how this charm just grows!
With every hug that I receive,
A sparkle helps me to believe.

A clumsy dance ignites the night,
With my jewels shining bright.
Who needs a crown when you can sport,
A funky gem that's quite the sort?

So, let's adorn our goofy ways,
With treasures from our silly days.
We'll giggle as we strut and sway,
In a sparkling, silly ballet.

Jewels of the Soul

In the box, a treasure hides,
With twinkling gems that never bide.
Every jewel, a silly tale,
Of moments grand and moments pale.

From plastic pearls to shiny rocks,
Fashioned from our playful knocks.
Each piece whispers a joke anew,
With every clasp, a laugh ensues.

So let's wear these funny charms,
Adorning life with sweet alarms.
In this collection of delight,
We'll shine like stars, oh what a sight!

Grab a gem and join the fun,
A sparkle race has just begun.
We'll dazzle in this merry spree,
With jewels bright, just you and me.

Links of the Heart

Linked together, cheek to cheek,
With every charm, our laughter peaks.
In this circle, joy is found,
With every giggle, we astound.

Wearing chains of silly dreams,
Sprinkling life with goofy themes.
A wobbly link, a twirl and spin,
With each connection, we break in grins.

Oh, links that swirl like ice cream cones,
A hodgepodge of our funny bones.
In a dance of cheer and glee,
Let's make our hearts sing carefree.

Let's bond and laugh; we're quite the team,
With jingly charms that brightly gleam.
Together in this wacky art,
Gems connect us, heart to heart.

Ornaments of Our Bonds

With ornaments that shine so bright,
We gather under twinkling light.
A goofy grin, a beaded twist,
In our bonds, nothing's amiss.

Each trinket holds a memory,
Of silly times, just you and me.
With every clasp, a laughter cue,
In this treasure hunt, we pursue.

We dance around like shiny dreams,
In a world, bursting at the seams.
With colorful beads that tell our quest,
In friendship's game, we're truly blessed.

So deck us out in silly flair,
With jewels that flutter through the air.
Together in this merry race,
Our hearts, entwined, find joyful space.

The Poetry of Rings

Rings that twinkle, oh so bright,
They spin and dance in morning light.
Found in a cereal box, who knew?
A charm for hearts, a whimsical view.

Some are shiny, some quite dull,
Lifting spirits when words are null.
A doughnut ring can steal the show,
With sprinkles bright, it's good to go!

Each one tells a silly tale,
Of snacking dreams on a steam train rail.
What's on finger? It's hard to tell,
A laugh, a sigh, or a donut shell.

So wear them proud and wear them wide,
No need to hide, just enjoy the ride.
In this funny game of love's embrace,
It's laughter we want, not just a trace.

The Patina of Passion

Oh, the rust of love is quite a thing,
A color splash—just like a ding!
Patina grows like peanut butter,
It spreads and sticks; it's quite the clutter.

In kitchen drawers, we often find,
Keychains and coins, all intertwined.
A crumpled note from '93,
Says 'I love you; please agree!'

Love can age like a fine old cheese,
With each weird smell, the heart agrees.
Imagine kissing a cheese plate, oh dear!
It's funny to think what we hold near.

So let's embrace the marks of time,
In all our quirks, we find the rhyme.
With every wrinkle, a story grows,
In silly ways, our passion flows.

Moments Captured in Gem

A gem of a moment, so they say,
Captured bright in a funny way.
Like cat videos or food that's hot,
Our best memories, but forgot to jot!

A diamond sparkles just like gum,
Chewing through life, who has the fun?
Histories bound in light and cheek,
Like wearing stickers—unique and sleek!

Got a sapphire from a toy machine,
A treasure found in a cold cuisine.
"It's worth a fortune!" we proudly claim,
With silly grins, we play the game.

So gather up these snaps of bliss,
In laughter and joy, we'll reminisce.
Each moment bright, a gem we wear,
In our hearts' vault, beyond compare.

-Adventures in Affection

Let's play a game, oh, what a ride,
With silly dares, we'll never hide.
Hearts can race at an ice cream stand,
When sprinkles fly from an eager hand.

We'll climb a tree and build a fort,
With pillows stacked, it's our support.
But then we slip and tumble down,
And roll like clowns across the town.

Chasing dreams on a bicycle spree,
Pedaling fast, just you and me.
Who knew love could be this fun?
With every laugh, we've already won.

So here's to all our wild pursuits,
In every heart, a pair of boots.
Adventure awaits in every bend;
In laughter and love, we find a friend.

Strings of Sentiment

In a world of twinkling beads,
I fashioned jewels with silly deeds.
A cranky pearl, a laughing stone,
A string of giggles—my heart's own throne.

With charms that dance upon my chest,
Each gem's a tale, a funny jest.
Like mismatched socks, they tell their part,
Worn proudly, these strings of sentiment art.

The ruby's blush, the sapphire's grin,
Each twist and turn, where to begin?
They clink and clank with every sway,
Creating laughter throughout the day.

So here's to necklaces of jest,
Their quirks, I wear, I am truly blessed.
With every laugh, a memory starts,
These shiny strings that warm our hearts.

Enchantments of Endearment

In a shop of oddities, I found a thread,
With bubblegum pearls and a pickle's head.
I strung them together, a sight most rare,
An enchantment crafted with silly care.

Each charm a story, a giggle, a tease,
With a jester's cap made from soft cheese.
They jingle and jive, causing a stir,
A magical chaos, making hearts purr.

So here's a charm that sings like a cat,
While another has whiskers and looks quite fat.
With laughter woven in every part,
These charms of joy sprinkle love in the heart.

Adorned in whimsy, these treasures glow,
Bringing a chuckle wherever we go.
In quirky designs, friendships do bloom,
With endearments wrapped in laughter's room.

Radiance of Remembrance

In a box of trinkets, I found a gem,
A glowing smile, just like our friend.
It whispered tales in a jazzy tone,
Of dance-offs had, of laughter sown.

Each shimmer recalls a humorous plight,
Like that time we danced under the moonlight.
A rhinestone giggle, a sparkle of cheer,
Reminding us how friendships adhere.

With silly pendants that wobble and gleam,
They hold the essence of our wild dreams.
As memories twinkle in shades of bright,
They radiate joy, pure delight.

So cherish these tokens, as odd as they seem,
Each bead tells a tale; each string is a theme.
In laughter's embrace, we forever stand,
With remembrance brightening life's grand band.

Cords of Kinship

Tangled together, like shoelaces tight,
Our quirks are the fabric that makes us bright.
With charms that wiggle, and laughter ensues,
These cords of kinship banish the blues.

A sparkling donut, a bouncy shoe,
A friendship forged in flavors anew.
With giggles in stitches, we tie each strand,
Creating a circle, hand in hand.

Mismatched beads tell our tales so well,
From epic fails to where we fell.
With every knot, we weave and spin,
Reminding us where our joy has been.

So here's to the bonds that keep us whole,
Crafted with laughter, a playful goal.
In the tapestry of life, we play our part,
These cords of kinship wrap around the heart.

Radiance of Remembrance

In my drawer, what do I find?
Beads and trinkets, all intertwined.
Some have stories, some just shine,
Should I wear them? Well, that's divine!

Uncle Joe's gift, all shiny and bright,
Did he really think it was a delight?
It looks more like a fish in despair,
But hey, it's fashion; I won't really care!

A charm that's shaped like a rubber duck,
I wore it once—just my luck!
People chuckle, give me a stare,
At least I know I don't have a spare.

Each piece holds laughter, a giggle or two,
Stories of mishaps, both old and new.
So I'll parade my bling out on display,
As we all waltz, in a funny ballet!

Glimmers of Hope

A necklace bright, oh what a find,
Sparkling gems but oh, how they bind.
They're laughing with me, in a funny race,
Who needs a mirror? I love this place!

My aunt thought this was chic and bold,
But it screams 'fashion' from ages old.
If pearls could talk, they'd hide in fright,
I wear my flair with pure delight!

One bead is chunky, another too rare,
They dangle like a wild dance affair.
Each twist and turn is a silly cheer,
A gala of jangles for all to hear!

So here's to the gems, so oddly styled,
That make me feel like an impish child.
With laughter they shimmer, never too far,
Glimmers of hope, shining like a star!

Tokens of Timelessness

This pendant claims to time travel quick,
But honestly, it feels like a trick.
Each bead a relic, a chatty friend,
'Wear me now,' they say, 'to the end!'

There's a piece my sister used for a prank,
She swore it sparkled better than rank.
If only it knew what it's been through,
That second-hand shop made quite a brew!

An ancient locket, with memories rife,
Holds nothing more than a laughing life.
Each clink and clatter tells tales of yore,
Of messy dinners and family lore!

So let's toast to treasures, quirky and neat,
That dance with us in this funny seat.
For every token tells stories anew,
Timeless in laughter, and that's how we do!

Stories in Silver

A silver chain that's twisted and bent,
Holds tales of mischief—oh, what a scent!
Each charm like an echo from back in the day,
Whispering laughter in its own way.

There's one shaped like a shoe—quite bizarre,
Did I ever wear it? Not to a bar!
Friends burst out giggling whenever I flaunt,
My fashion statement, a curious haunt!

With each little bead, a smile ignites,
Worn during dances and silly fights.
They giggle and jingle with every sway,
As I trip in style, come what may!

So here's my collection, as odd as can be,
In a world where laughter is key.
Each piece sings stories, forever in tune,
Silver smiles sparkling under the moon!

Locket of Love's Echo

In the pocket of my heart, a locket lies,
A picture of my cat, in a cute disguise.
Next to a donut, oh what a sight,
Even my heart giggles, what a delight.

It jingles when I dance, oh what a sound,
A meow and a laugh, all around.
With every step, it bounces and sways,
Spreading joy in the silliest ways.

Every crush I've had, I store in this case,
A key to a memory, filled with grace.
But mostly pizza, because it's a laugh,
This locket's a keeper of my silly gaff.

So here's to the treasures, big and small,
In my quirky locket, I cherish them all.
From love to laughter, this bond I maintain,
Forever storing joy in a funny refrain.

Shimmering Bonds

Oh, shiny things, how you make me smile,
With sparkles and giggles, you're always my style.
A bond that glitters, a charm that's bright,
Laughing at life, oh what a delight!

From silly charms shaped like a fish,
To a heart that's actually a disco dish.
Every giggle we share, it brightens the day,
Shimmering moments that simply won't fray.

Connected through laughter, like links in a chain,
A sparkle of friendship, never mundane.
Each jingle and jive brings a carefree cheer,
With shimmering bonds, there's nothing to fear.

Together we shine, in this jovial dance,
Twinkling each moment, oh what a chance.
In this laughter-filled world, let's never depart,
With shimmering connections, we're never apart.

Links of the Heart

They say love's a chain, though mine's a joke,
With links made of laughter, and a funny cloak.
Each person I meet adds a silly ring,
Creating a chorus that makes my heart sing.

From quirky friends who dance like dorks,
To chatting with squirrels and other strange folks.
Each link in my heart, it clangs and it chimes,
Composed of our giggles and the best of times.

I've got one for my mom, it's shaped like a pie,
Another for pizza and a wink of the eye.
Each clink and each giggle, a story we share,
In this lighthearted life, love fills the air.

These links of connection, both funny and bright,
Make every dull moment burst into light.
In the whimsical world where my heart thrives,
Each link is a giggle that happily survives.

Echoes of Connection

In the hallway of hearts, there's a laughter spree,
Rings echo and bounce like a bumblebee.
With each silly joke, a connection we weave,
In the fabric of fun, we truly believe.

From dad jokes to puns, they never grow old,
With echoes so sweet that simply unfold.
A chorus of laughter, a whimsical start,
The song of connection that hums in my heart.

In this funny little dance, we wiggle around,
Creating a symphony that's joyously sound.
Resonating giggles, like bells in the park,
Our bond sings with echoes that light up the dark.

So here's to those moments, so quirky and bright,
With echoes of fun that feel ever so right.
In this amusing adventure, let's play our part,
With laughter as music, we'll dance from the start.

Harmony in Gems

In a world of sparkle and shine,
Rings on fingers clink in time.
Earrings dance like silly sprites,
While necklaces laugh, oh what a sight!

Brooches wink with cheeky glee,
'Look at me, oh can't you see?'
Jewels play hide and seek with light,
In this treasure chest of pure delight!

Charm bracelets jingle a happy tune,
Gems gossip under the light of the moon.
'You wear that shade? It's simply divine!'
They giggle together, oh how they shine!

Glitzy gatherings, laughter unconfined,
With every piece, stories intertwined.
Adornments full of whimsy and cheer,
In the realm of gems, joy draws near!

Opalescent Memories

Once, a pearl tried to start a trend,
Wore a beret, thought it was the end.
Shells were laughing, what a sight!
In a sea of style, such a fright!

Gems retold tales of clumsy days,
Amethyst bumbled in purple haze.
'Just a slip!', she giggled with flair,
'I still shine brighter, I just don't care!'

Rubies red with grace, took a bow,
'Fashion's easy! Just ask me how.'
As diamonds rolled their sparkling eyes,
In opalescent hues, well, who needs ties?

Laughter echoed around the fold,
Every gem, a memory to hold.
In the jewelry box, stories reside,
With every sparkle, a smile can't hide!

Charisma of Connection

In the charm of glitter and glitz,
Neat stacks of earrings make funny fits.
'Why wear one when two can play?'
'In this sparkle war, I'll save the day!'

A bracelet whispered, 'Let's unite!'
'Together we shine, oh what a sight!'
With a wink and a twinkle so sly,
They formed alliances, oh my, oh my!

Rings rolled out in a joyous parade,
Each gem glimmering, never afraid.
'Catch me if you can!', they all sang,
As the laughter and the memories sprang!

Connections gleamed, twinkling bright,
In this merry gem party, pure delight.
With every chuckle, bonds intertwined,
In a world of glimmer, love was defined!

Ties that Bind

Strung along in a colorful line,
Gemstones chattered, feeling just fine.
'You're too bright!' said the shy little stone,
'But with laughter, we all feel at home!'

A quirky chain sparked a big trend,
'Ties that bind,' it said, 'no end!'
With clips and clasps like a funny crew,
Together they laughed, 'What else can we do?'

A bead with a grin whispered, 'Join me!'
'In this colorful chaos, let's merge and be free!'
As laughter erupted in twinkling delight,
They danced through the darkness, shining bright.

With every piece found, a new friend in sight,
Connecting hearts in a joyful flight.
In shiny shenanigans and moments divine,
These ties that bind are simply sublime!

Vows in Varieties

In a store with shiny things,
I spotted some bling, oh what joy!
A heart-shaped charm, a sparkle or two,
Pick one to please your favorite boy.

I wore it at noon, it clinked, it danced,
People gathered, they laughed with glee.
'Is that a necklace, or a cat's new toy?'
I shrugged, 'What's the difference? Let it be!'

With beads that jingle and glittering stones,
Each gift's a giggle wrapped in surprise.
I'll wear them all, or just when I choose,
Like fashion statements spoken in sighs.

So gather your gems, your quirky delights,
Strap them on tight or let them hang free.
Each vow we make is a twist in our lives,
Full of laughter, oh let's just agree!

Lovelinks

In a box topped with lace, my treasures await,
A curious mix, both shiny and bright.
Some look like fish, and others like cakes,
Each link a joke that gives me delight.

In a fridge, I found pendants of cheese,
Displayed with flair, like a birthday treat.
Friends walk in, and they chuckle with ease,
'Is that dairy fashion? You can't be discreet!'

Colored strings, a mishmash of dreams,
Worn round my wrist or upon my breast.
Each twist and each turn brings giggles and beams,
With lovelinks that truly outshine the rest.

So wear your oddities, let others compare,
Life is too short to wear what is plain.
Wrap hearts like candy, show off your flair,
In this whimsical game, we've all got a gain!

Ties of Traditions

Grandma's brooch, a broil of odd charms,
A quirky tradition for family ties.
Though it wobbles and wiggles, it certainly warms,
Stories it holds are as big as the skies.

A cousin's creation, it hangs like a kite,
Crafted from buttons and glitters galore.
'Is this a necklace or styling miswrite?'
Yet wearing it proudly opens new doors.

In gatherings, giggles, and hearts in a knot,
Each piece tells of laughter, of gaffes too sweet.
Inherited chaos, a rainbow of thought,
Ties of traditions, now who's feeling beat?

So let's celebrate what makes us all grand,
Find joy in the jest of our family crest.
Each trinket a handshake, a wave of the hand,
In this merry-making, we're truly blessed!

Treasures of the Heart

In a treasure chest filled with mock gems,
Lies a collection of trinkets so wild.
Each oddity gleams like forgotten hymns,
Worn by the bold and the curious child.

A shovel charm, cleverly designed,
'For digging my way through love's boundless mess!'
Even rubber ducks, all so inclined,
To float in the ocean of happiness!

Bracelets of laughter, they spin and they twirl,
Knowing full well that the joke's on us.
For each shiny thing that can make a heart whirl,
We wear them with pride, and we honor the fuss.

So gather your treasures, your giggles and grace,
Each piece tells a story crafted in fun.
In the end, it's all about love's embrace,
Like a necklace for hearts, we shine as one!

Fragments of Forever

In a box of old trinkets, a wild squirrel danced,
Gleaming charms fell off, oh how they pranced.
They giggled and jiggled, on a sunbeam they'd float,
Dreaming of a world, where each gem held a coat.

A paperclip shined, saying, 'I'm really gold!'
While buttons from jackets took stories untold.
They whispered of laughter, shared memories so sweet,
Amongst all the chaos, they jived to the beat.

The rubber band stretched, claimed, 'I am the king!'
An odd pair of socks joined in for a fling.
With each twisted trinket, a tale came to play,
Laughter echoed as they danced through the day.

Underneath the sunlight, they sparkled with glee,
Hoping a kind heart would come set them free.
Secrets of romance, stories broad and bright,
In this quirky gathering, love took its flight.

Adorned with Affection

In grandma's old jewelry, a war broke out,
Rings argued like warriors, full of clout.
Ear cuffs tossed insults, with the loudest rings,
While brooches debated who could fly with wings.

A locket chimed in, "I hold love so tight!"
But a necklace replied, "I sparkle so bright!"
Each charm donned a hat, or a feather to wear,
The pearls rolled their eyes, "Fashion's a dare!"

"Let's check the mirror," a bracelet now cried,
As the pearls all rolled off, in a colorful slide.
With laughter and jests, they gave quite a show,
Dressed in fond memories, they'd steal every glow.

They laughed 'til the sunset cast shadows on gold,
Whimsy in heirlooms, love stories retold.
In a treasure chest, they felt ever so grand,
Adorned with affection, a frivolous band.

Bejeweled Emotions

A gem in my pocket said, 'I'm sad and blue!'
While a shiny old quarter sang, 'I'm rich, yes it's true!'
A clasp piped up, 'Hey, let's not fight today!'
For each little treasure, has feelings at play.

The bangles all chimed, 'We jingle with joy!'
As the brooches exchanged tales, no need to annoy.
The emerald felt green, it yearned for some fun,
While the sapphire declared, 'Let's bask in the sun!'

A ring looked perplexed, 'Am I in a wrong mood?'
The necklace just chuckled, 'Don't be such a prude!'
In this bejeweled circus, emotions ran wild,
With laughter and antics, every gem a child.

Together they sparkled, like stars up above,
Dancing and twirling, a spectacle of love.
Who knew this shiny bunch could giggle with zest?
In the world of adornments, they truly were blessed!

Heirlooms of the Heart

An old cufflink grinned, it knew all the tricks,
Reminiscing the dance floor, 'twas quite the mix.
While a locket turned, saying, 'I hold the past!'
In a whirlwind of fashion, these moments were cast.

Buttons from blouses began a small fight,
Declaring their worth under the spotlight.
One said, "I'm classic!" with a prideful stance,
While zippers added flair, insisting on dance.

The keychain exclaimed, 'I unlock all your dreams!'
The sparkle in each gem shone bright like moonbeams.
With heirlooms adorning the fabric of days,
Their whimsical stories made laughter a blaze.

As night fell upon them, they whispered with heart,
Creating a narrative, each playing a part.
In the treasure of memories, emotions would spin,
For every old relic had a story within.

Keepsakes of the Soul

In a box of treasure, wonders glow,
A rubber band from school, who'd know?
A friendship bracelet, frayed and fun,
Happiness tangled, all in one!

A button from a coat, lost in the fray,
Each item a story, come what may.
A tiny toy dinosaur, all chipped and old,
Reminds us of laughter, a tale retold!

Old tickets to movies, a nostalgic cheer,
A note from a crush, "Will you hold my beer?"
The glue that binds, all mishaps aside,
These quirky keepsakes, oh what a ride!

From funky bow ties to socks that don't match,
Each piece a reminder, none hard to catch.
Souls intertwined in silly displays,
A treasure trove of memories, endless arrays!

Orbs of Affection

Round and shiny, they giggle and spin,
Full of laughter and the joy within.
A marble from childhood, it winked at me,
Saying, "Life's a game, let's play with glee!"

A balloon animal dog, deflated and worn,
Yet it barks out joy, a memory born.
A bouncy ball sings when tossed in the air,
Tickling our hearts, bringing us flair!

The rubber duck squeaks, in bubbles it plays,
In the bath or the pool, it brightens our days.
A silly emoji that rolls with delight,
Orbs of affection, shining so bright!

Dancing disco balls glow with pure glee,
Inviting us all to forget the debris.
These playful wonders, they twirl and they wink,
Orbs of affection, bringing smiles as we think!

The Tapestry of Together

In a quilt made of memories, colors align,
Each patch stitched with laughter, oh so divine!
A swatch from a party, where we all danced,
Or a coffee stain from the day we pranced!

Weave in the moments, the tickles and cheers,
The silly mishaps over the years.
A thread of a joke that never grows old,
The fabric of friendship, warm and bold!

Frayed edges of time, oh what a sight,
Each laugh a thread, holding us tight.
Button-eyed teddy that always knows how,
Together we're stronger, the 'why' of the 'how'!

So grab a piece, add your own flair,
In this tapestry woven with love and care.
With each stitch a giggle, a fumble, a quirk,
Our absurd creation, a playful perk!

Symphony of Sentiments

Clashing cymbals, a chaotic tune,
Heartstrings strumming, like a happy cartoon.
A trumpet that toots for a dessert we shared,
Each note tells a story, hearts laid bare!

A xylophone's giggle, like rain on a roof,
Each drop of sunshine, just look at that goof!
A group of friends dancing, off-beat but free,
Creating a rhythm, oh, can't you see?

The bass line rumbles with all of our grins,
An encore of laughter, where humanness wins.
A funny little ditty, we all sing along,
A symphony of sentiments, our hearts in a song!

So grab your kazoo, let's make some noise,
In the concert of life, everyone enjoys.
With beats that are silly and lyrics absurd,
Together we laugh, let our spirits be heard!

Mementos of the Mind.

In a drawer filled with treasures, so rare,
Lies a jumble of laughter, a whimsical flare.
Each trinket a chuckle, a giggle or grin,
Tales of our blunders, where do I begin?

There's a spoon from the diner, remember that day?
When I spilled all the ketchup and sighed in dismay.
A pebble from hiking, my shoe came untied,
The falls were all worth it, with friends by my side.

A rubber band slingshot, oh what a delight,
It launched every paper plane, took flight every night.
And the cap from a soda, my drink turned to foam,
Yet still, in these moments, I felt right at home.

So here's to the mishaps, the jests we hold dear,
Each item a memory, brings laughter and cheer.
In the wild world of memories, let's not be apart,
For every silly moment creates mementos of heart.

Gems of Connection

In my pocket I found a lost button friend,
Stitched paths of laughter, humor won't end.
A mismatched sock from the laundry's embrace,
Combined with a laugh, it adds style and grace.

An old game of charades, oh what a scene,
When I mimed a tomato, and you guessed it as green!
Each word was a giggle, a wink, and a tease,
Through ridiculous moments, we do what we please.

From silly fridge magnets to fridge art so wild,
These gems of connection, they leave us beguiled.
For it's not just the glitter that makes our hearts shine,
But moments together that spark joy, pure and fine.

So treasure the laughter, the quirks, and the plays,
Life's jewels are moments we'll cherish always.
In this collection we find, as we sip and we part,
Every gem strengthens bonds; they're a map to the heart.

Adorning Souls

With each little giggle, we all start to glow,
Collecting our quirks like a fabulous show.
An umbrella of memories to dance in the rain,
Adorning our souls with the joy and the pain.

There's a hat with a feather from last summer's bash,
Worn askew with a grin, we stirred up quite the clash.
The wig from the party made everyone gape,
Turning serious moments to sheer comic shape.

A paper crown worn, so regal yet wild,
Queen of the giggles; oh, life is beguiled!
Each item a ticket, to moments we wear,
For fun is the fabric of friendship we share.

So let's don our adornments, in colors so bright,
With laughter and joy, we'll shine day and night.
In this circus of life, we find our true role,
For each silly charm is what adorns the soul.

Threads of Affection

In a quilt made of laughter, stitched by the past,
Each thread tells a story, quirky and vast.
From mismatched socks to a rubbery band,
Our threadbare affection, it's nothing but grand.

With a cup full of coffee and crumbs all around,
Every spill and each giggle is laughter profound.
A wiggly dance when the music goes low,
Celebrating the chaos, embracing the flow.

So here's to the memories, both silly and sweet,
In our patchwork of friendship, we weave and we greet.
The knots and the tangles make stories collide,
For within threads of affection, our hearts will abide.

So let's tie all the threads, with laughter as glue,
Every bump in the road gives color anew.
Together we laugh, through thick and through thin,
In the fabric of friendship, our joy shall begin.

Traces of Love's Journey

In a box of mismatched trinkets,
Lies the fondest of memories.
A crooked ring from that trip,
Lost in sand, just like our keys.

Marbles from a childhood game,
Swirl of colors, fun to chase.
Each one tells a different tale,
Of laughter, tears, and a funny face.

A broken bracelet, quite the sight,
But it sparkles in the light.
Reminds me of that clumsy dance,
With two left feet, no second chance.

Love's journey marked by silly things,
Who knew hearts could wear such bling?
With each mishap, a spark of glee,
These trinkets hold our history.

Glistening Testaments

Broken bits of shiny stuff,
A charm that's lost its luster,
Yesterday's joy, today's little fluff,
It still shines, despite the muster.

A glittery star that missed its lease,
Found beneath the couch, no doubt.
A treasure from a hungry feast,
Where crumbs and laughter danced about.

These pieces tell the tales we share,
Of foolish deeds and heartfelt plight.
From silly fights to loving care,
Each sparkle bears our shared delight.

So let's wear them like a crown,
These glowing slips of our past.
With every giggle, ups and downs,
Our love's a riot, built to last.

Emblems of Emotion

Doodles of love drawn on the fridge,
Sticky notes and lost cheerios.
Each faded piece, a little smidge,
Of laughter wrapped in warm shadows.

A rubber band, oh what a find!
Bouncing memories with each twang.
In its simplicity, love entwined,
A stretchy smile that always sang.

A paperclip shaped like a heart,
Holding together all we've said.
In moments funny, we won't part,
Our jokes and giggles, love's own thread.

Emblems of emotion, swirls so grand,
Tiny relics of our play.
In this treasure chest, hand in hand,
They dance and laugh, come what may.

The Heart's Adornment

A button from your favorite coat,
Still tells the tale of wind and rain.
Stitched with laughter, there's no remote,
To rewind that ride on the train.

A hairpin that holds stories tight,
Of how you danced when you thought you'd fall.
Its twinkling gleam in the pale moonlight,
Marks the missteps that began it all.

A lost tooth from a daring bite,
Later found under the couch's sway.
It brought us giggles late at night,
In memories that forever stay.

So let us wear these tales so dear,
Each piece, a laugh, a tear to start.
For life's just better when we cheer,
With all our quirks, it's pure art.

Glimmers of Intimacy

In the closet, gems reside,
Each with a story, they won't hide.
A sparkle here, a twinkle there,
Worn with laughter, light as air.

Chasing glitter down the street,
Strangers stare at my wild feat.
Who knew a brooch could play such tricks?
A dancing brooch? It surely sticks!

Earrings chiming like a song,
Matching socks? We don't belong!
A crystal here, a feather there,
Fashion's folly, what a affair!

Rings that jingle with delight,
Joyful chaos—what a sight!
My jewels laugh, my outfit sings,
In this madness, bliss it brings!

Emblems of Embrace

Bracelets jingle on my wrist,
Each one tells of friends I've missed.
A charm for each embarrassing tale,
Worn with pride like a badge in fail.

A giant hoop, I could take flight,
Or trip and fall, oh what a sight!
They catch the wind and swirl about,
Spin me 'round, I twist and shout!

Necklaces stacked like a tower,
Gems that droop but still have power.
Wearing them while I bake a pie,
Hope they don't catch fire—oh me, oh my!

But in a hug, they settle down,
Giving comfort, never a frown.
With every clasp, a giggle spark,
Emblems of joy, lighting the dark!

Whispered Wishes

On my necklace, dreams align,
Whispers of joy, like sweet red wine.
Charm after charm, a tale unfolds,
Each wish whispered—a memory holds.

A star-shaped pearl, a laugh, a grin,
Worn upside down, where to begin?
Twinkling jests fly with the breeze,
Caught in laughter, longing to tease.

My clasp once broke, a tale of woe,
As diamonds rolled like icy snow.
Chasing sparkles down the stair,
Those wishes danced without a care!

But in my heart, they're shining bright,
Crazy jewels that feel just right.
In every slip, my dreams ignite,
With whispered wishes, pure delight!

Treasures Within

Oh, buried deep in my old chest,
Lie treasures mocking my wild quest.
There's Grandma's brooch, a worn-out key,
And what's this thing? A rubber tree!

A trinket shaped like a funky fish,
Hoping to grant my every wish.
Gems that glitter but choose to hide,
With silly faces, laughing wide.

In each odd piece, a tale to tell,
Navigated through life's funny swell.
Lost earrings like ships seek the sea,
Their stories twist; they're wild and free!

So here I stand, a treasure chest,
In this kooky game, I'm truly blessed.
Just like my jewels that seem to spin,
The laughter shines, and joy falls in!

Tandems of Tenderness

Two hearts ride bikes, oh what a scene,
With helmets askew and smiles so keen.
Pedals go round, but where's the brake?
Laughter erupts, oh what a mistake!

Side by side, they giggle and race,
Chasing each other, just making haste.
Tangled in chains, they twist and collide,
But nothing can tear their joy aside.

Bananas and apples, snacks in the sack,
A shared little picnic when spirits lack.
Silly stories and winks they exchange,
Hearts dancing wildly, nothing feels strange.

Together they bounce like rubbery balls,
Falling in puddles, oh how one sprawls!
Yet each splash brings a burst of delight,
In tandem they soar, oh what a flight!

Crystalized Connections

In a world of glitter, they try to impress,
With baubles and bobbles, and some fancy dress.
But the sparkle's not in the jewels they wear,
It's the quirks they find, in moments they share.

Two mismatched socks, a sight to behold,
Yet linked by their laughter, a bond pure gold.
A dance in the kitchen, a slip and a slide,
They chuckle together, with glee they abide.

Wobbly tea cups and crumbs on the floor,
A friendship like this needs none to adore.
With every failed recipe and crazy test,
The glimmer of joy shines, it's simply the best.

Through crystalline dreams and shapes quite absurd,
They cling to each other without a word.
A toast to the fun, let the glasses clink,
With laughter that bubbles, they never sink!

Echoes of Affection

In a crowded café, a spilled cup of Joe,
Turns into giggles that steal the show.
Sipping on chaos, their hearts intertwined,
With every mishap, more joy they find.

Whispers and secrets, like echoes they share,
Bumping their heads, oh, what a flair!
Sentences jumbled, like pasta gone wrong,
Yet every weird moment turns into a song.

Through comic mishaps, love grows with ease,
With awkward high-fives and scoops of cheese.
They dance with the rhythm of a quirky beat,
Twirling in sync, oh what a treat!

In the echoes of laughter, their spirits delight,
With each silly joke, everything feels right.
Like candy confetti that fills up the air,
Their bond is a melody, a charming affair.

Sentiments Encased

In a jar of giggles, they capture the day,
Mismatched emotions all jumbled in sway.
With notes on the fridge that twist and remind,
Of silly inside jokes that tickle the mind.

One's in a tutu, the other in shoes,
Whirling around like a pair of goofballs,
They dance on the couch, making quite a scene,
Dreaming in colors, vibrant and keen.

They share their odd dreams while baking bizarre,
Creating sweet muffins that look like a star.
With flavors so wild, and frosting so bright,
It's a sweet kind of madness that feels so right.

In the jars of their hearts, sentiments tucked tight,
Every messy moment is pure, pure delight.
With goofy embraces and playful retorts,
Their love story sparkles, with endless supports.

Charms of Our Journeys

We wandered far with goofy hats,
Collecting tales and silly chats.
With every step, a charm we find,
A story shared, laughter intertwined.

Adventure calls, let's take a ride,
With snacks in hand, and hearts open wide.
Tangled maps and missed out cues,
But every detour feels like good news.

In this treasure hunt, we're quite the team,
With footprints etched like a wild dream.
Stumbling through, our giggles soar,
Each step a giggle, wanting more!

So grab your charm, let's walk this trail,
With silly tales we'll never fail.
Together we shine, in colors bright,
Our journey's laughter, a pure delight!

Beads of Belonging

Each bead we string tells a tale,
Of silly nights that never pale.
We gather round with puns so sly,
In our little circle, no need to be shy.

With mismatched shoes and wild hairdos,
Creating chaos, sharing our views.
Every laugh, a bead in the mix,
Together we're bound by fun little tricks.

These funky beads, they dance and sway,
A memento of friendships that won't fray.
In every color, a memory's glow,
Celebrate life with beads in tow!

So raise your glass, let's make a toast,
To all the moments we cherish the most.
With every bead, let's tell our dreams,
In laughter and joy, nothing's as it seems!

Opals of Sentiment

Opals gleam with a silly flair,
Reflecting moments we all share.
Each one holds a giggly plot,
From mishaps to fun that can't be bought.

We dance around with glee and cheer,
Creating memories we hold so dear.
With our strange quirks, we shine so bright,
Every opal a laugh, a loving sight.

In puddles of giggles we take our dives,
With goofy grins, we come alive.
These opals twinkle, a playful light,
Warming our hearts, oh, what a sight!

So gather 'round, let's share our tales,
In a world where laughter never fails.
Opals of sentiment, wild and free,
Together we dance in pure jubilee!

Chains of Compassion

We link our hearts in laughter's chain,
With jokes that spark like crazy rain.
In silly moments, compassion flows,
Where friendship blooms and true care shows.

Every link's a hug, a hearty cheer,
Holding us close, keeping us near.
Laughing through storms, we find our way,
In our merry band, come what may.

So if you trip, we'll catch your fall,
With jokes and laughter, we'll have a ball.
Chains of compassion, gleaming bright,
In every stumble, we find delight!

With hearts linked tight, we'll dance and play,
Creating memories every day.
A playful crew with our hearts set free,
In chains of compassion, we'll always be!

Chains of Kindred Hearts

In a world of quirky ties,
Friendship's charm never dies.
Each bead a tale, each link a laugh,
Silly moments on our behalf.

With glittering gems that twinkle bright,
We wear our stories day and night.
An oddball mix, but that's the art,
Crafted with joy from the heart!

Sometimes tangled, but never apart,
Each knot a giggle, a work of heart.
A jangle here, a jingle there,
Life's fun when you're with that pair!

So let's dance with beads and gold,
Our laughter louder than tales of old.
In chains so vibrant, silly, and sweet,
Together forever, we can't be beat!

Reflections in Gemstone

Look at this glimmer, so strange and bright,
A quirkier gem is quite the sight!
With a swirl of colors, a laugh in its gaze,
We shine through the silly, in the oddest ways.

A ruby's blush, a sapphire's grin,
Diamonds that giggle, where do we begin?
Rings of laughter, bracelets of cheer,
In this playful world, there's nothing to fear.

Reflection shows us, a funny old crew,
Winking back at the zany things we do.
In the sparkle and shine, see our wild grace,
Each moment a spark, a joyful embrace.

So toast to the gems, a merry parade,
In a kaleidoscope life, let's never fade.
For every facet tells a tale, it's true,
In the mirror of fun, it's just me and you!

Whispered Wishes

In a world stitched up with sincere wishes,
Silly dreams dance in fishy dishes.
Whispers of laughter float on the air,
Crafting our bond, a whimsical pair.

Each wish a spark, a glittering cheer,
We shout them out loud; we've nothing to fear!
From wishing wells to chocolate bars,
We find our magic in among the stars.

A whimsical world of wishes untold,
Where dreams don't wither and hearts grow bold.
With giggles and joy in abundant supply,
Our fun little wonders can never run dry.

So gather your hopes, let's make 'em a race,
With a whirl and a giggle, let's float to a place.
Where whispered aspirations fill the air,
And shimmer with laughter – a delightful affair!

The Love That Shines

The glimmer of giggles, from pals so dear,
Our love shines brightly, never unclear.
With a flash of fun and a wink in our eyes,
We wear our affection like a comical prize.

From playful banter to silly delights,
We craft our moments as stars in the nights.
With every chuckle that rolls off our tongues,
A symphony of laughter, forever young.

Hearts decked in humor, like jewels on display,
We spread joy around, come what may.
In the tapestry woven with giggles and gleam,
Love is our spark, the fun is the theme.

So let's toast to the love, a radiant beam,
Shining with antics, a whimsical dream.
Together we twinkle, forever aligned,
In a dance of affection, so sweetly confined!

The Locket of Longing

With chains that jingle, oh so bright,
I lost my locket, what a sight!
It landed in my soup one day,
Now it giggles, what can I say?

The cat plays with it, sets it free,
It rolls around, a merry spree!
My search is like a treasure hunt,
For a trinket that likes to taunt.

With every turn, it gives a laugh,
In my pocket, it took a bath.
It makes me ponder, where could it go?
To sparkly lands beyond the glow?

So here's my wish, oh locket dear,
Stop hiding, and just come here!
For every heart is full of grace,
But yours is always hard to chase!

Pendants of Promise

I bought a charm, it promised me,
That with its magic, I'd feel free.
Instead, I found it stuck on tight,
It dangles on my bag, what a fright!

My friend said, "Wear it, it's a joy!"
But now it sings, like a toy!
With every jiggle, my heart skips,
This pendant turns into strange quips.

"Bring me luck!" I whispered low,
Instead, it brought a circus show!
It dances, chuckles, on its chain,
A jokester in this jewelry lane.

So here I flaunt my pendant bold,
A promise wrapped in stories told.
For every whim can bring a cheer,
In this wild world, let's laugh, my dear!

Heartstrings Entwined

Two strings of hearts, they twist and bind,
But mine just tangled with a pine!
I wore my charm to serenade,
Yet in the trees, my necklace swayed.

It caught a bird! What a delight,
Now it sings a tune, day and night!
The neighbors frown, "What's that noise?"
"Just my jewelry, and its poise!"

With every flutter, each sweet chirp,
My heartstrings dance, they twist and burp.
I chase it down, a playful chase,
Who's wearing who in this odd race?

So here I stand, a tangled heart,
In nature's grasp, we play our part.
Let laughter echo, winds can't part,
For love's a knot, a joyful art!

Adornments of the Spirit

Adorned in colors, bright and loud,
I dress my spirit, feel so proud!
With beads and baubles, what a sight,
But trying to dance? What a plight!

They jingle-jangle, make me wobble,
I trip on dreams, oh what a trouble!
My bracelet sings a catchy tune,
While I just stumble like a goon!

I ran to spin, to show my flair,
And landed in a big ol' chair.
Now all my gems are in a heap,
They giggle softly, 'Tis no leap!'

So here I twirl, a festive mess,
With every spin, I confess:
For joys of spirit can be wacky,
But make me smile, and feel less tacky!

www.ingramcontent.com/pod-product-compliance
Lightning Source LLC
Chambersburg PA
CBHW070313120526
44590CB00017B/2665